one woman's testimony

I WAS DEAD, NOW I AM ALIVE

AIDAH N. NAKASUJJA NSEREKO

I Was Dead, Now I'm Alive
© 2012 by Aidah Namayanja Nakasujja Nsereko

All rights reserved. No part of this book may be reproduced or transmitted in any form or by any means, electronic or mechanical, including photocopying and recording, or by any information storage and retrieval system, without permission in writing from the publisher.

Published by
Deep River Books
Sisters, Oregon
http://www.deepriverbooks.com

ISBN- 13: 9781937756031

ISBN- 10: 1937756033

Library of Congress: 2012941824

Printed in the USA

Cover design by Joe Bailen, Contajus Designs

Dedication

This book is dedicated to my Savior, Jesus Christ. Throughout my entire life, He has always been there for me. He is the reason I am able to write this book to give an account of my life and walk with Him.

Acknowledgments

First, I want to thank God for opening the way for me to write this book and bringing all the information contained within it to its completion and publication. Next, I am thankful for my mother and father, who brought me into this world and taught me the virtues of being a God-fearing woman.

I am also very grateful for the financial and emotional support of my husband, Mr. David Nsereko. I thank Pastor Simeone Kayiwa for his spiritual support during a time when I desperately needed it; your prayers made it possible for me to accomplish my mission. Additionally, I appreciate the level of support many friends and relatives provided during the development of this book.

The presence of Anna Nabukenya and Edward Ssentongo blessed me tremendously as they—for the sake of the kingdom of God—carved time out of their schedules to lend their moral and physical support to bring my book to its publication. I want to also express my gratitude to Dimitila N. Lubega for such genuine kindness and invaluable support when I desperately needed it.

I would like to register my gratefulness to Hope Studio, who recorded the voices from which this manuscript was transcribed. The enemy tried hard to frustrate the exercise, but God prevailed.

Last, but not least, I am grateful for the management and staff of Deep River Books who, by the inspiration of the Holy Spirit, propelled this book to what it has become. May God continue to bless you abundantly!

Table of Contents

Dedication 3
Acknowledgments 5
Preface 9

CHAPTERS

1   A Stranger Within Me 11
2   Commotion in the Salon 13
3   How God Fashioned the Universe 15
4   A Sea of Grace 17
5   Worthless Trappings 19
6   Outer Worlds 21
7   The Fourth World: Heaven 23
8   Heavenly Treasure 25
9   Back to the Salon 27
10 Namirembe Christian Fellowship 29
11 The Voice of Someone Across the Sea 31
12 Mysterious People 35
13 Incomplete Task 37
14 Beautiful Stream 41
15 Beautiful Flower 45
16 Angry Children 51
17 Pipes & Telephones 55
18 How Prayers are Handled 57
19 Repeating Prayers 61
20 Heavenly Mansions 65
21 A Taste of the Gehenna Fires 67
22 Abraham's Palace 69
23 Threadlike Bridge 73
24 Children Perishing 79
25 The Highway 81
26 Heavenly Monitors 91
27 The Final Call 93

Epilogue 95
Remarks 96
Biography 96

Preface

This nonfiction book confirms scriptural teaching regarding the existence of heaven, hell, eternal life, and death. In particular, it details Christian living, which leads to heaven or hell and what exists within each realm.

There have been many near-death and actual death experiences during which people have confirmed the existence of a divine dwelling place. The events outlined in this book, however, do not contradict or corroborate any heavenly experiences. They uniquely chronicle my experience when I briefly died and my spirit ascended to heaven.

While in the company of the Lord Jesus, I was given a heavenly tour and a hellish exploration into death and destruction. This vivid experience is clearly a message to be shared with the world. This is, indeed, the purpose for which my heavenly Father has placed me on earth.

Writing this book was not a straightforward experience; accessing resources to develop it could not have happened but by the grace of Almighty God. People have many questions about the eternal kingdom of God and life after death. More specifically, what occurs in heaven and hell?

Although most Christians have an overarching belief about eternal life and death based on Bible scripture, believers and non-believers grapple with whether or not there is actually an eternal realm. Most people cannot conceive a vivid picture of what either realm resembles.

This book is a response to pertinent questions people have about the afterlife and what humans need to do in order to live a full life of righteousness through Jesus—the way and truth. He is the One who ensures eternal life (John 14:6); this fact aligns with biblical teachings.

As told through the spiritual eyes of Aida (my authentic self), the existence of the Holy Trinity—God Almighty, Jesus Christ, and the Holy Spirit—are confirmed. Hopefully, this account of my experience will richly bless readers to open your spiritual eyes and ears to living a Christian life to fully prepare for the eternal kingdom.

God loves the world so much He does not desire anyone to perish in hell. This is the reason He sent His only begotten son, the Lamb of God, who died for the forgiveness of our sins, that whosoever believes in Him may have eternal life (John 3:16). He calls us to surrender all our hearts' burdens to Him, so He may shoulder them and lead us to a special place (Matthew 11:28).

May God bless each of you.

Chapter 1
A STRANGER WITHIN ME

Praise the Lord, brothers and sisters. I thank God for the gift of life, for it is truly wonderful. This truth I know all too well.

At mid-day on November 16, 2006 I had an actual death experience. As evidenced by the fact that I authored this book, the Lord breathed new life into me.

I had not been sick on this particular day. In fact, I was seated in a hair salon when the incident occurred. I progressively started to feel dizzy then an indescribable sensation intensified as I started to black out.

I noticed what appeared to be two people within me. As this phenomenon continued, I tried to determine the identity of the second person.

"My, God," I prayed aloud, "What's this?"

This second person resembled me and perfectly fit every inch of my body. Then, she slowly stepped out of my body. As she was leaving my body, I realized she was my authentic self. Aida was her name.

Aida was my inner person, who was invisible yet very real. In other words, my physical body was a tailored dress, which God created to house my inward, true self. I later learned my spiritual self slowly emerged and detached from my physical body and living being.

I was eager for my spiritual self, who I refer to as the Spiritual Aida, to be removed from my body entirely. However, I soon realized her urgency to transition outside of my flesh as well.

Spiritual Aida methodically traveled up my body from my lower extremities, moving from my knees, past my neck and mouth, ultimately reaching my nose.

She systematically separated herself from every area of my body—my hands, fingers, joints, etcetera. Her detachment from my physical being resembled the parting of a hand from the inside of a glove.

Finally, Spiritual Aida aligned her eyes and mine. As she gazed outside my body, I sensed my eyes transforming into those of a dead person. Yet I was very much alive.

She remained in my body, the sensation of her presence eventually settling in my forehead. At this point, her entire being transformed—from her legs to her head—to fit squarely inside my forehead.

Chapter 2

COMMOTION IN THE SALON

There was a commotion as the customers who were seated around the salon began shouting, "She died!"

I saw them all. My mind was alert and I clearly understood everything that was happening. People panicked, and some scooped up their belongings and scurried out of the salon.

One lady, who quietly observed what was happening, drew closer to where my body lay to help save my life. However, her efforts were unsuccessful.

She lifted me into her arms and called out to whoever could hear, "Please, come and help me!"

Then a woman emerged from a nearby room, followed by another patron. The sight of these ladies was, indeed, the last thing I recall as the commotion in the salon continued.

Chapter 3

How God Fashioned the Earth

I started ascending and was no longer conscious of any earthly activity. Instead, as I felt myself ascend, I witnessed new things. I was able to fully behold God's creation: this world.

I was introduced to how God fashioned the earth with incomparable wisdom. The ends, pillars, and curves—everything which comprises and holds Earth together—were amazing.

Next, I saw the entire earth below was filled with gross darkness; yet, it was noon. It was riddled with filth and terror—all nations, without exception. In some places, people were being beheaded; in others, people were worshiping all manner of false gods.

Prostitution ran rampant, airplanes and buses crashed, and blood flowed everywhere as people were fighting and killing one another. From the distance, I observed evil filling every corner of the world.

I wondered: *How can we live in this kind of world?*

Chapter 4
A SEA OF GRACE

In the midst of the chaos and bloodshed, there was an amazing, extraordinary grace hovering over the world. This grace was so immense it was comparable to a sea of water covering the four corners of the world. God's tremendous grace enabled people to live in such a dangerous and vile world.

I have often heard believers say: "Lord, give me the grace to…"

There is enough grace for each person to become, do, and achieve whatever God has planned for their life. There is enough grace for all people in the world to be saved, and walk in holiness and righteousness. There is enough grace for every person to go to heaven.

Many people, however, do not know that this grace is abundantly available to them so they do not fulfill God's purposes for their lives. Instead, they continually ask God to give them the grace He has already made available. I perceived God will eventually take away His tremendous grace; every person will be required to save and take care of themselves.

Chapter 5
WORTHLESS TRAPPINGS

I continued moving toward the outer edges of the world. I asked myself: *What good is in this world?*

When I tried to find good or precious things in the world—things of great value and riches which people crave—they turned out to be rubbish. I thought: *Everything seems to be rubbish!*

People kill in order to obtain the things of this world. Some people even abandon God to acquire things. If only they knew the filth and worthlessness of such things.

As I proceeded onward, I thought gold might be an exception—I soon realized it was no different. Acquiring material things is not a bad objective, but it pales in comparison when measured against the value of attaining the eternal things of God.

Gradually, I developed a hatred for everything in this world because I could not see anything of true value. Instead, I saw a world filled with cheap treasures incomparable to eternal life in and the treasures of the kingdom of God.

Chapter 6

OUTER WORLDS

As I traveled farther, I entered another world, a second realm. This second world was completely dark with a concrete, tangible darkness. I could see and touch it.

As I touched it, I said, "This darkness is unbelievable."

I continued moving upward, until I came to the end of this dark realm. I entered yet another world, a third realm. This sphere was filled with a bright light, a very bright sun. It was beautifully adorned with precious heavenly things.

This spectacular world was similar to a place where a grand or royal wedding was being hosted. Every area was covered with gold, silver, and sparkling white. Big tables were arranged similar to those at a wedding reception. Well-decorated, there were no earthly words to describe it—it was beyond description.

I was surprised I did not see a single living creature in this world. Not even a heavenly angel.

Chapter 7

THE FOURTH WORLD: HEAVEN

I reached the fourth world: heaven. It was a dreamlike place where God lives and it was blue in color.

It dawned on me—I had truly left Earth. I put my hands on my head and cried out, "Oh no, I was not prepared to come here! Lord, how did I get here?"

As I continued to marvel in reverent fear at my new surroundings, a great, wonderful, marvelous treasure was revealed to me. I later learned that I possessed this treasure, and it was the reason I was able to get to heaven. This treasure was brighter than one thousand noonday suns. I was able to behold it with my naked eyes, as clearly as I could see a person standing next to me. This marvelous treasure represented being in the presence of the Lord Jesus and walking after Him.

When I saw this treasure, I wondered why it had not been revealed to others. Why wasn't anyone talking about it? I perceived that a lot of the time preachers talk about worldly treasures and riches but never this kind of treasure.

The value of this particular treasure is immeasurable. Those to whom it has been revealed are far richer and wiser than others on earth. Believers who have access to this treasure have the greatest wealth and riches in heaven and on earth. This treasure exists in all those who accept Jesus Christ as their savior, constantly walk with Jesus, and have the manifestation of the fruit of the Holy Spirit because they have invited Christ to abide in them and they in Him. They are known as the salt and light of the world (John 15:1–5 KJV, Matthew 5:13–14).

After surveying the treasure and staring at its beauty, I perceived I was actually one of those who had accessed it. I found it hard to believe.

I exclaimed, "Lord, how is it I have been chosen to have this kind of wisdom?" It was revealed that all the chosen who agree to walk with Jesus Christ are guided by the Holy Spirit and therefore have access to Wisdom—not as the world gives, but as the kingdom of God gives—and, therefore, access to all the treasures in heaven. These heavenly treasures are the fruit of the Spirit: love, peace, joy, kindness, humbleness, goodness and others. Anyone who walks with Christ is eventually transformed to live here on earth as in the eternal life, with love for the Lord as well as for one another, kindness, a peace that surpasses all understanding by human standards, and to bask in the joy of our strength, our Lord. (Galatians 5:22–23 KJV)

Access to this treasure reaffirmed, yet a third time, that I am one chosen by God. I was extremely pleased and slapped myself to see if I was dreaming. I was not experiencing a mere dream. I was in heaven; a place filled with indescribable joy and happiness.

Chapter 8

HEAVENLY TREASURE

Once this treasure was obtained, my soul became one of the billionaires in heaven. As a result of the opportunity to experience a taste of heaven, I saw many things. My travel was abundant—I swam in treasures of peace, happiness, joy, and love. While I was swimming in these treasures, I discovered an abundance of gold in heaven's vastness. Within its kingdom is the city of gold, which is surrounded by a high wall. Heaven is arranged in well-maintained, beautiful compounds.

Wisdom permeates the heavenly realm; even grass intelligently understands its surroundings. Earthly wisdom is so narrow it simply cannot be compared to heaven's comprehensive wisdom. The vast beauty of heaven is incomparable to anything here on earth.

After discovering this great treasure, I went farther. I saw *Life*. The life I discerned appeared to be real, visible, and clear.

Rhetorically, I asked in awe, "Can life be so vivid and tangible?"

As I drew closer, it filled heaven's canvas and I actually touched it! When I touched life, it penetrated my entire being. I was no longer myself; I became life itself. I was filled with life, to the deepest core of my being.

I went farther and encountered *Peace*. Like life, peace was so real I truly could see and touch it. I ran towards it to confirm its realism. When I reached out to touch peace, it also permeated my entire being. Once more, I was no longer myself, I became peace. Every inch within me was covered by peace like snow or dew covering a mountain.

I continued on and met *Joy*. I touched it to determine its authenticity. As I touched joy, it was equally incredible. It, too, filled my being to the extent that I felt nothing, except sheer joy.

I was no longer just Aidah; I was filled with life, peace, joy, riches, and every good thing imaginable. It is in knowing Christ and abiding in Him that every good thing you can ever think of—from the smallest to the greatest—is accessible to you.

Heavenly treasures—life, peace, joy—are exceedingly good. No earthly expression can measure up to or describe these treasures.

Next, I came upon a certain place which appeared to be a lake. This was a lake of life, peace, and joy.

I said, "Lord, this life is wonderful!"

I jumped into the lake as if I was diving into a swimming pool. I swam in a lake of inexpressible euphoria.

I thought to myself: *How did I survive in an evil world?* I reflected and remembered some of the things on earth, which caused me to nearly fall into a spiritual death. As I contemplated how I escaped, I realized I had received the kind of wisdom to save me. I thanked God.

Then I heard the Holy Spirit say: *Aida, although you have left an evil world, there is a task you were supposed to complete, which you didn't.*

I tried to resist and deny it. I said, "I can't go back. I have safely arrived here. I will remain here. I am not going anywhere."

This voice inside me, the Holy Spirit of God, did not say anything further. So, I continued to bask in my life-filled, peaceful, and joyful heavenly treasure.

Chapter 9

BACK TO THE SALON

Let me digress back to the hair salon where this experience unfolded. I was later informed that at three o'clock on the afternoon of my death, four patrons remained with my body. They were moved by my sudden death and tried to determine what to do, where to take my body.

Some people emerged from neighboring businesses, sensing there was something wrong at the salon. The four women handling my body would not discuss anything with these observers. They had collectively agreed not to disclose or announce the death of someone in the salon at this juncture.

The group decided to take my body to the hospital for a post-mortem examination, then return to the salon to announce my death. One of the women hired a special taxi, which parked directly in front of the hair salon. They placed my body inside the waiting taxi and sped off.

However, no sooner had the taxi started to travel some distance than a mechanical problem occurred. The taxi would no longer move.

The small group of women became panicked and confused. They tried to stop passing cars for assistance. However, when passersby asked what the problem was, they displayed my dead body inside a car. Naturally, people were scared, reluctant to help, and drove away.

This situation continued for quite some time. By now, the taxi driver had lost his patience with the small group's dilemma. He demanded, "Remove your corpse from my vehicle. I want to go. I have been patient with you long enough."

In the midst of the small group's dispute with the taxi driver, five female evangelists on their way to evangelize appeared. When the women saw the small group's distress, they came to their aid.

Chapter 10

NAMIREMBE CHRISTIAN FELLOWSHIP

The evangelists quickly recognized me as one of their fellow church and choir members at the Namirembe Christian Fellowship Church. So they decided to push the taxi to Pastor Kayiwa's Namirembe Christian Fellowship. Pastor Kayiwa was in his office with a few people.

Upon arrival, the women immediately lifted my body out of the taxi. Before they reached Pastor Kayiwa's office, women who had been outside his office immediately rushed to tell him a dead body had been brought to him. He did not move from his chair.

He simply continued his work and told them, "Let them wait a bit."

My body was eventually taken into Pastor Kayiwa's office. During this lapse in time, someone went to my home to notify my mother about what had transpired. By now, she had arrived at Pastor Kayiwa's office.

Chapter 11

THE VOICE OF SOMEONE ACROSS THE SEA

When Pastor Kayiwa began to pray, I heard him from heaven. I heard him as if he was a parent calling his child.

He said, "You come back!"

I thought: *Let me see who exactly is calling me, then I will quickly return.*

As soon as I had decided to do this, I immediately connected with the voice calling out to me. The voice gained energy and force, pulling me at a terrific speed.

As rapid as a lightning bolt, the voice pulled me billions of miles from where I was. When the pastor called a second time, I fell from heaven's blue world. When he called, yet a third time, I passed back through the spectacular world full of light and staged for a wedding. Next, I descended through the world of darkness.

Finally, when he called me a fourth time, I re-entered this world. During my descent, I saw people gathered around my body—my mother, friends, brothers, sisters, and the women who had escorted my body to Pastor Kayiwa's office. I heard every word spoken, while some sobbed and others wailed.

My mother cried, "Lord, my daughter, my daughter!"

When I heard her voice, I was rather jolted, wondering: *What are these people crying about?* I could not perceive why anyone would cry for me especially since I had been taken to a better place than this world. Obviously, they would have had to have been in the spiritual realm I had been in to realize that it was not necessary to cry for me but rather rejoice that I was in a better place.

It was really strange to see people cry for me. My eyes shifted away from them. I returned to see who called for me then my plan was to ascend back into heaven, quickly.

A nurse from Mulago Hospital was in the pastor's office. Although the office had been closed to prevent interruption from people gathered outside, I had the ability to effortlessly move through roofs, doors, and concrete walls; I entered Pastor Kayiwa's office. The people inside his office did not sense my presence.

In heaven, I was spotless. However, when I viewed my body laid in the pastor's office, the dress I was wearing was filthy. I was grimy and impure.

I realized I needed to re-enter the dress (my physical body) in order for everyone to recognize me. Putting on my dress, I realized Pastor Kayiwa had been the person calling for me. He was aware I had returned to my body.

"Help me lift her up," he said, operating in the Spirit realm.

Once he lifted my body, he hugged me then I heard my inner person, Aida, receive authority to remain on earth. At this moment, I became sad because I wanted to return to heaven immediately. I believed it was the best place for me.

If you recall, when I initially entered heaven, I was told about an earthly task I needed to complete. I remembered this admonition and understood I had been given another opportunity to perform my assigned task. So, I settled down.

It took awhile for the people in the office to realize I was alive. They called in people who had anxiously monitored events from outside Pastor Kayiwa's office. Everyone scurried in to see what had happened.

I heard and saw everyone clearly—not with my physical ears and eyes, but with my spiritual ones.

People exclaimed, "Pastor Kayiwa has revived her. Miracles of born-again Christians are real, quite real!"

They were all happy and excited, then they lifted me up.

One person asked the pastor, "Should we take her to the hospital?"

He responded, "It's not necessary."

I was given several glasses of water. At this point, I was not able to swallow the first few sips I took. However, by my third glass of water, I was able to swallow normally.

The pastor directed, "Give her a little more."

So, they gave me more; they were very happy.

Then Pastor Kayiwa said, "Take her back to her home."

The driver who had been at odds with the women, demanding my corpse be removed so he could leave, had not yet left the church. Even the women who had rushed with him to drop off my body at the church remained.

I was carried back to the hired taxi driver's vehicle and driven home. The car ran smoothly. It was as if the taxi had never experienced a mechanical failure.

Chapter 12

MYSTERIOUS PEOPLE

One thing was very unclear; I could not recall whether angels or other beings had helped return me to my earthly body. I recall that when I re-entered my body I could not properly fit into its frame.

My body was wrinkled, dry, and had hardened. When I attempted to place my spiritual hands back into my physical hands, it felt similar to pressing my hand through a brick wall.

When I detached from my physical body, every part of it had become as hard as a rock. After my return, I saw people (or angels) boiling water. They placed a towel in the water and started massaging my body with it. Every area they placed the towel softened.

I re-entered my hands, legs, joints, and every other area of my body's softened frame. Slowly, I refit perfectly into my physical body.

After I came back to life, I felt lighter like a piece of paper that even the wind could easily carry. My skin remained gray for some time. I could neither feel cold nor hot. You could have boiled hot water at the highest temperature and poured it on me and I would never have felt anything. That went on for almost a year.

After I had been refitted into my body, for some time I was still able to perceive two people within me.

At times I would ask people, "Can't you see the two people within me?" They acknowledged they only saw one person.

So I insisted, "Listen, as I bend down."

For whenever I bent over, my physical body would first bend, followed by my inner person, making a slight cracking noise.

I asked, "Can't you hear I'm two-in-one?"

This particular phenomenon lasted for about one month. Now, I no longer sense two people residing within me.

Chapter 13

INCOMPLETE TASK

I reconciled that the main reason I am still alive is because I had not completed the task God created me to do in this world. While in heaven, I found I was not the only person who had not completed His divine assignment. I saw many people who had done nothing to fulfill their God-given assignment.

Many had already ascended into heaven while others still lived on earth, their divine assignment still incomplete. The actual task God created me to do was not confirmed until my 2006 ascension into heaven. However, it was first revealed to me in 2000.

Different churches held overnight prayer services which I frequented on a regular basis. One night, the Lord spoke to me saying, *"Go whenever there are prayers because your brothers and sisters are also there."* So, I made it my business to know when and where overnight prayer services were to be held.

Since such prayer services were held once a week in our church, I often attended other overnight prayer services. On one particular day, I felt tired and decided not to attend overnight prayer; I wanted to sleep.

While I slept, I heard a man's voice calling out to me around three o'clock in the morning. This was the voice of the Lord Jesus; I knew His voice.

"Here I am, Sir," I responded.

He said, *"Come over here."*

I watched myself wake up, arise from the bed, and go over to Him. He was dressed in a beautiful blue gown. He held my hand and we started walking.

I realized that when the Lord came for me he left open what appeared to be a door or huge gate to heaven. We walked towards the open door (or gate) hand-in-hand.

When we walked through the doorway, angels guarding the opening closed it behind us. As we moved beyond this heavenly gate, I saw something resembling an airstrip. Then I saw four kinds of winds tasked with bringing air into its due season. These four winds are talked about in Jeremiah 49:36 and Revelation 7:1. Whenever these winds blow, a wonderfully sweet fragrance fills heaven.

As Jesus and I continued our walk, we came across gardens of flowers with no apparent end. The various flowers were beautifully planted in sprawling rows.

When we reached them, they bowed down and worshiped the Lord in unison. These flowers produced wonderful songs and melodies, similar to a skillfully played piano. They bowed to one side then toward the other in an orderly pattern, praising and worshiping the Lord.

I watched in delightful awe and wanted to pick some of the flowers. As living creatures, these flowers intuitively understood what I was planning to do. They started to draw away from me, swaying back and forth. Although an intelligent life-form, these flowers also have angels who guard them. Just like we humans operate here on earth in an orderly departmentalized fashion, in heaven every department has a group of angels tasked with protecting and running that department. In this case, angels were tasked with protecting the flowers in heaven. Most especially, the angels are there to be in service to humans in heaven just as they do here on earth for those that are heirs to salvation in heaven (Hebrews 1:14).

Then Jesus guided me to another area where I saw trees bowing and worshiping God. Like the flowers, these trees are planted in an orderly fashion. I also came across various beautiful stones which worship and praise God.

No human being on earth sings praises to God like these little stones. They sing with incredibly sweet voices, making a melodic sound like flowing water.

As we continued to move forward, Jesus and I came across a very large heavenly courtyard. I realized this courtyard was comprised of different departments with angels working in each of them. Unfortunately, some departments have not been worked in since they were established.

The angels who manage these departments are idle because they have no work. I was walking alongside the King of heaven; therefore, these angels could not come close to us.

They called out, "We have no work; we have never worked."

This is when I came to understand that believers generate work for heavenly angels to perform. When we do not activate them, angels do not work.

As we continued to pass through, I realized everything a person needs is contained within each of these departments. God established them to fulfill man's needs.

We approached a section in this huge heavenly courtyard where I saw fierce angels like no other. They are tough, giant fighters who do not tolerate anyone manipulating the things of God. They stand on these words: As it was, so it is, and forever it will be.

Their responsibility is to execute and enforce God's decrees. To be considered their friend, one has to stand on God's word, as they do.

These angels have different sizes, ranks, and assignments. Some are so tall they almost touch the sky. Some are as broad as ten feet. Some represent a variety of human sizes. Yet, each angel enforces God's orders.

As we approached them, I saw something near them and wanted to carefully examine it. In heaven, everyone is respected. Even if a job is as lowly as cleaning toilets, sweeping roads, or cleaning chairs, the person assigned a duty is highly respected as is the divine task they perform.

Jesus left me to approach these angels.

As soon as I made a move to head towards them, one of the angels stopped me saying, "You are not supposed to come this way."

The angel's voice lifted me up with great power and at such an accelerated thrust; it threw me quite a distance away. I fell down.

When I lifted my eyes, I found other angels looking at me. They allowed me to rest a bit, as I was exhausted and overwhelmed. Once I recovered, one of the angels touched my hand and led me back to Jesus.

Jesus did not say anything to me; He simply touched my hand and we moved on. Jesus is governed by His word, even if He is the One who established it. His word so governs Him that He cannot do anything outside of it.

From my heavenly perspective, I observed earthly believers praying to Him day and night to help them with various things. However, these people were not operating under His word, which meant heaven was not able to help or fight for them because they were living outside of God's word. I saw angels eager to come to their aid, to give them what they wanted, but they could not.

These angels observed, "If only these people would operate under the word of God, they would see what we are capable of doing."

Angels are eager to help, but people are not aligned with heaven, heaven cannot war on their behalf. That is, not until they fall back under God's word; this is when they will be helped.

Chapter 14

BEAUTIFUL STREAM

As I continued walking with Jesus, we came to the city of God at the center of heaven. God's city is enclosed in a fenced wall, with no apparent end to its height, length, and width.

The two of us entered the city where I saw a beautiful river of clean waters covered with glass. This stream surrounds the entire heavenly realm, including the throne of God Almighty.

When I saw this stream, I wanted to frolic in its beautiful splendor. I pulled my hand from Jesus' and ran towards this stream. Jesus slowly followed behind me. When I reached it, I asked myself: *How did this stream really come into being?*

In heaven, there is no need to ask questions because whatever is asked is clearly revealed. I understood this stream originates from the seat of God, from the throne of God Almighty. As I drew closer to examine it further, I saw that the water begins as a thread from the throne of God then becomes progressively larger until it develops into a huge stream surrounding heaven. I also saw a river of milk from the throne of God, not from a cow.

After I saw these things, I drew closer to the seat of God, which is made with incredible wisdom and precious riches. No human words can describe it. The seat of God is simply beyond my limited comprehension.

So, I decided to play in the beautiful stream. Again, as intelligent beings, these living waters understood what I was planning to do. So, they withdrew from me. Whenever I ran towards this water, it would draw away; whenever I stopped, it ceased to withdraw.

Eventually, I conceded and an angel escorted me back to the seat of God from the stream. I was eager to take a second look at God's seat to examine its front portion.

As I approached the front of God's seat, I saw precious things beyond words. There was a very beautiful flower which flows with God's inexpressible beauty; it surrounds the base of the entire throne. Other flowers flow with what appeared to be honey.

I digress to emphasize God's beauty which falls like snow off a mountain cap. His beauty tangibly changes like lightning. Meaning, no one exactly knows, understands, or captures His essence, let alone is able to describe Him.

He is everything. Whatever He is, He envelopes it entirely and absolutely. God's honor also is beyond description. It is like snow. This honor runs throughout heaven.

There were sounds similar to bombs, but they were not threatening or frightening. The sound is incredibly beautiful to the ears. Some are like heavy clapping of hands while others mimic jazz and different melodies. Still, there are so many others.

I continued listening to the beautiful sounds of heaven, realizing colors of heaven changed every second. They captured different colors, thereby, making it extremely hard to concretely describe heaven's beauty. It is, quite simply, exceedingly beautiful and wonderful.

The stream is bright with red and golden colors. The red color represented the blood of Jesus. As I drew closer, an angel working in this department emerged from behind me and threw me into this stream. As I laid in it, I bobbed up and down; it was exhilarating.

As the angel took me out of the stream, Jesus immediately came to me and said, *"Aida, have you seen this stream?"*

I responded, "Yes, I have seen it."

Then He said, *"That is the stream of My blood."*

Then He told me something I did not expect. He said, *"You're going to return to the world and tell all the people if they repent, there is blood to purify them."*

He paused adding, *"The problem is they don't want to repent, but go and tell them to repent. There is blood to purify them."*

I received confirmation there is no sin that cannot be washed away by the blood of Jesus Christ. Every kind of sinner who genuinely repents, however wicked this sinner may be, the blood of Jesus will purify him completely.

Shortly thereafter, Jesus told me about a person on earth who was contemplating repentance. This is how it works: every thought, since we began to perceive right from wrong and understand God (around seven years old), has been heard and registered in heaven. Moreover, every word we have ever spoken has been heard and registered in heaven as well. Every whisper we have ever uttered, even in darkness, has been heard and registered.

When a person on earth conceives a thought, heaven quietly listens to the thought. Everything done on earth, heaven sees as clearly as one can see through a glass of clear water.

So it was, when a woman thought of repenting of her sins, in heaven we knew where she was located in the earth. She was in her garden dressed in a multi-colored dress with a flower print. She was pruning her plantains.

Once she made her decision to repent, the angels responsible for washing away her sins immediately swung into action. They made preparations to cleanse her.

They cleansed her even before she began repenting in her garden. I was greatly surprised and wondered: *They start cleansing her even before she repents?*

The woman finished working in her garden, went back to her sitting room, and started repenting. However, in heaven, she had already been washed clean and dressed her in white garments.

When I saw this situation unfold, I was extremely happy. I thought: *How easy it is to repent? You simply decide to in your heart and it's done!*

Moving to another side of God's throne, I happened upon another stream. This one was very bright with silver colors. In the middle of this stream was a man dressed in white—I understood Him to be the Holy Spirit.

I tried to draw closer to study Him more carefully, but I could not. He was filled with an intensely bright light. I stood still, gazing at Him for a moment.

Jesus said, *"Aida, have you ever seen Him? He is the Holy Spirit. You are going to go back to the world and tell the people to trust in the Holy Spirit. He will help them with their problems because He is available to help them."*

After pausing, He added, *"But why don't they believe in Him? Go and tell them to trust the Holy Spirit to help them with their problems because He is available to help them."*

I realized the Holy Spirit was grieving because people would not allow Him to work in their lives.

Chapter 15

BEAUTIFUL FLOWER

As Jesus and I continued our tour, I saw a flower which had been planted by Jesus. This flower is surrounded by rings of heavy metal, securely protected. It sprawls like monkey grass around its metallic ring and the throne of God.

I was reminded of one day long ago, when God, Jesus Christ, and the Holy Spirit decided, "Let's create a special creature, and make it number one in position by comparison to all creatures and put it in our midst." When they looked around heaven at all the creatures, riches, and precious things at their disposal, they selected this flower.

Surprised to learn this, I asked, "How was this flower selected among all things?" I perceived that this flower represented man who was by the grace of God redeemed from the curse of bondage to sin, brought on earth by Adam and Eve's disobedience. "For God so loved the world that he sent His only begotten son…" (John 3:16 KJV).

This flower was not the best, but they chose it. After choosing it, they loved it so much, injected it with their riches, treasures, goodness, and beauty. Meaning, this flower has everything it needs to live fully or abundantly.

As I admired the flower, it began to change. I fell in love with this flower as God had. It was extremely beautiful with wonderful green leaves. All of a sudden, the flower changed colors, turning grey before my eyes.

Some leaves took on the appearance of those on plants eaten by insects, or the leaves of a tree experiencing a prolonged dry season. They were filled with holes or covered with dry patches.

Most of the leaves were peeling off. What few leaves remained lost their original green coloring. Some leaves had withered, only small dry stalks remaining.

I felt a terrible sadness and began to weep as I gazed at what happened. Jesus said, *"Aida, what's wrong with you?"*

I responded, "Lord, do you see this flower?"

He turned His eyes towards it then asked, *"So, you have also seen it?"*

Then He said, *"I loved this flower so much and I filled it with all my riches and treasures."*

As Jesus spoke these words, He raised His hand. I looked up and saw His throne was empty. The only thing that remained was His seat and garment. He had put everything into this flower.

"I put all my life and treasure into this flower, but time is almost running out. I'm about to close the door," He said, explaining that the flower represented His church.

The leaves are the people, yet most of the leaves had fallen off the flower similar to leaves that have fallen off trees and have been scattered. Some leaves were punctured with holes while others had dried out. However, there are those with life remaining on the flower, but have lost their green coloring.

Jesus said *"This is My church, but there is still more. Come and see."*

We went to another side of God's seat and He pointed. *"Look."*

Every leaf represented a person on earth. Now, take a moment to consider which of the following leaves described represent you:

Are you one of the leaves that fell?
Are you one of those eaten up by insects?
Are you one of those which have lost their original coloring?
Are you one of those left with dry stalks?
Are you among those leaves punctured with holes?
Are you one of the leaves that maintained its greenness?

Once again, Jesus pointed, saying, *"Look,"* as we moved to yet another side.

When I looked down, I saw the Church of Christ. Everyone was asleep—the Church of Christ was in a deep sleep.

Jesus said, *"Do you see them? They are dangerously asleep. When I call out to them, they don't hear. When I speak, they don't hear. When I walk in their midst, they don't understand."*

I stood beside Him as He called out to His children. His voice is deafening, like a roar.

He called out again urging, *"My people!"*

His roaring voice exploded across the world as a reverberating echo. Every creature on earth, including the foundations of the world shook; the seas and lakes folded; the mountains disappeared. Every creation on earth, including the smallest specimen, heard His voice and responded with reverent fear. Except, however, the sons and daughters of men, who did not move one inch. They could not hear His voice. I was bewildered by this.

Jesus directed, *"You are going to go back to the world and awaken My church."*

Believers are asleep in a dangerous way. Moreover, the hearts of man are completely sealed. I liken this sealed heart to metal welded to metal. This frightened me, as I saw people's hearts hardened.

I argued, "Lord, I cannot go back to the world."

I saw the work He was sending me to do; it was too hard. If Jesus, who has such a powerful voice to move seas and fold mountains, could not move human beings, why on earth would such people ever listen to me?

I became scared and declared, "I will not go back."

There happened to be many angels in the place where I stood with Jesus. I pleaded, "Let these angels go in my place. I am not able. The world is very hard. Let one, two, three or four of these angels go in my place."

The Lord admonished me, *"Don't talk like that!"*

In the midst of our exchange, I found myself transported to yet another place. This time I was not alone with Jesus, I was in the presence of God Almighty, too.

The Almighty was not standing where we stood. Instead, He was above us. At first I could not hear what He was saying.

I was finally able to hear Him say, *"If the child goes back to the world and doesn't [complete her] work, she will fall."*

God wanted me to come back to the world to awaken His church in 2000. This is the task I had not yet performed on earth.

I received my instruction to come to say these words. However, when I returned, I did not say anything nor did I inform my pastor about it. It was not until 2006 when I had my death experience, and upon reaching heaven, that I was reminded there was an assignment I had not completed as initially instructed in my first encounter with the Lord in 2000.

I have a divine task. For this reason, I am still alive. You, too, have an assignment you must discover, acknowledge, receive, and complete. Ignorance of it does not absolve you. Every person will be asked to account for what they did to fulfill their divine assignment.

I learned the day a child is placed in his or her mother's womb is actually not the day he/she is created. Heaven revealed to me the souls of many children, who have not yet been embedded and are in a designated space. Such children eagerly wait for the day they will be placed into their mother's womb to be born into the world.

When the time comes, the souls of children in this space are selected for implantation into their mother's womb. On this day, a file is opened for each child. Written within this file are the divine tasks to be performed on earth, and how each task is to be accomplished.

Conversely, I saw the souls of children whose time of placement in their mother's womb had come, although their mothers refused to bear them. These children have lost hope of ever coming into the world to fulfill their God-assigned tasks.

I heard the children cry out, "Our mothers refused to bear us; we have no hope. We will not enter the world."

They tell fellow children who are not yet due, "At least you have a chance to go into the earth."

Even the souls of children who are not yet due for placement in their mother's womb have apprehension. Their mothers also may refuse to carry them to term for birth into the world.

When I was placed in my mother's womb, my assignment was given to me. At a certain age and an appointed time, it was predestined for Jesus to take me to heaven and reveal things for me to announce to the world.

You, too, have something God has assigned to you. Every person has been placed on earth for a specific purpose, to complete a specific mission. This is the reason you exist, to fulfill your divine assignment.

Many people do not complete their heavenly tasks. Instead, they make the choice to do their own thing. However, there is a day of judgment when every person will account for whether or not, and how, they accomplished their mission on the earth.

When I arrived in heaven, I found my divine assignment was to proclaim these words to the world. Initially, I did not release them because I was afraid. The world is not easy; people would find it hard to believe me.

When I returned from death in 2006, my pastor found out everything I had experienced. He then anointed me and told me to do the work God had assigned me to do. Well, here I am. This is the work I have been called to do at this appointed time. God predestined me to share the words contained in this book with the world.

Chapter 16
ANGRY CHILDREN

I also saw the souls of children who had been placed in their mother's womb, yet had been aborted. These souls are very angry. They are quite actually fierce and repeatedly accuse their mothers to God day and night, weeping before His throne.

Furthermore, I saw the souls of children who had been born, but died during the course of childbirth. Surprisingly, every soul knows its story—the cause of death and who was responsible—to give an account before God.

Moreover, I saw the souls of children who had died prematurely due to their parents' negligence, depriving them of a chance to live. These souls also accuse their parents day and night.

These souls ask God, "When will they come? Lord, when will you judge them?"

God replied, *"Wait; be patient."*

These souls recount what they saw while in the womb and outside in the world. Each story is narrated from the perspective of the age of the child at the time of their death, as well as according to the circumstances surrounding the event. The souls of these children range from two months in age to twelve years old. Every child has a divine task on earth.

Moreover, people already born into the world abandon their tasks, but the souls of children in heaven are anxious to enter the earth to perform their assignments. According to God's design, some believers start their divine tasks when they are young while others complete theirs well into adulthood.

We each are responsible for making a contribution to the advancement of God's plan, even before the fulfillment of our divine task. For me, I decided whatever I did before fulfilling what I was called to do, I would do it with all my heart.

I was a church choir member, an evangelist, and a prayer intercessor. I participated when we used to preach the Gospel in the villages, climbing mountains. I committed every resource I had access to towards the cause of the Gospel.

In addition, I participated in the hospital ministry and visited Uganda's Mulago Hospital to care for the sick. I used to walk to raise money to buy patients food to eat, juice to drink, and soap to bathe with or wash their clothes. Sometimes giving my own clothes, blankets, bed sheets, or whatever I had available to give.

There were hospital patients who expected me to visit each week. My visits reached a point when the nurses warned me, "You will contract diseases in this place." They gave me protective gear such as hospital gloves and garments.

I also used to participate in the church drama ministry. I often had the privilege of playing the main character in our theatrical productions. As a result of this ministry's work, many people were saved.

Although I had done all these good works, when I reached heaven I realized I had done practically nothing. Why? I had not performed the primary task for which I had been placed in my mother's womb; the assignment written in my heavenly file.

People often find themselves in a similar dilemma. Like me, they have wasted precious time. For instance, someone may be predestined to receive salvation at sixteen years old. However, they do not become born again until twenty-five years old. The angels in heaven record non-activity in this person's file from the time he/she was predestined for salvation until the time it was actually received because their life's trajectory altered movement toward his or her divine assignment. This person will never redeem time squandered.

Every page of our life's file is opened annually, then it is sealed. Each year the angels open a new page to record the tasks a person has fulfilled.

When I had the opportunity to examine some files, I saw many were empty. The angels simply crossed out pages because people had done nothing to complete their heavenly assignments.

Some people were practicing witchcraft; the years for them to perform their divine tasks had already passed. Others were involved in prostitution, while another segment remained in a self-indulgent state.

In other words, they had not pursued the purpose for which they were sent into this world. They did their own things. Yet the Bible says of the rebellious in Romans 6:23 and Ezekiel 20:13—their disobedience will lead to punishment in the form of eternal death!

I was among the rebellious. God sent me in 2000, but I did not do His work at the appointed time. Meaning, I, too, wasted a number of years. I cannot redeem the time, but I am now working to complete my assigned task.

It was only as I started executing my divine purpose that the angels started writing about active service in my file. I was concentrating on doing other things. The other things, such as caring for the sick, are referred to in heaven as *good works*. God is pleased with and rewards good works. However, these acts do not pardon us from judgment.

Many people do good works, not the primary task for which God created them. When a believer reaches heaven, when his or her file is opened, they will be asked why this task was not completed. After all, it is the major purpose for which he/she was created by the Almighty God.

As for me, I thank God so much for giving me another chance to rediscover and fulfill my divine assignment.

Chapter 17
PIPES & TELEPHONES

In heaven, I noticed a very huge pipe upon which many telephones were connected. Every one of us has a telephone connected to this pipe. As I approached the telephones to read the details concerning each owner, I realized each person's history is recorded individually on telephones.

This history outlines the reasons why we were born and captures everything in our lives that we have done and were supposed to do. Once more, many people have died without fulfilling their divine purpose.

As I examined these telephones more closely, I discovered many of them had never actually been used. An angel has been entrusted to care for each person and their heavenly telephone. Likewise, every person has his or her own pipe. Meaning, all of heaven expects to hear our prayers and these heavenly telephones capture each thought and every word ever spoken. These telephones serve as communication channels between heaven and earth. Sadly, most of these telephones have not been used.

Chapter 18

HOW PRAYERS ARE HANDLED

In Chapter 14, a lady who simply thought of praying was mentioned; in heaven we heard her clearly. We knew where she was located and what she was doing at the particular moment of her contemplation.

This lady actually began to pray. She started by wisely thanking the Lord; He was pleased. She then worshiped the Lord in wisdom; again, God was pleased. After she worshiped God, every being in heaven was quiet, waiting to hear what this lady was going to pray.

God was also listening. Jesus listened intently.

Rather than pray for something she needed, this lady said, "Lord, you are Lord. You are Lord. You are good and you've given me life."

She continued, "Lord, you are great. You are Almighty. You've done great things for me. You are the King of heaven."

She concluded by saying, "You are Lord. Indeed, you are Lord. There is none like you, not one."

Everyone was expecting her to pray about something heaven could do for her. However, she slowly said, "You are Lord, Lord, Lord, Lord…"

All of heaven was elated because it is very rare for a prayer to be lifted in this manner; a prayer able to reach heaven through her heavenly telephone. It is considered a miracle when heaven receives such a prayer; the angels of God rejoice.

Equally, sadness manifests because many prayers are prayed amiss and do not reach heaven. This is why heaven rejoices when a person's prayer successfully reaches its realm.

We eagerly anticipated her to pray for something specific following her penetrating prayer of wisdom. However, she did not ask God for one thing.

Although she praised and worshiped Him, she did not ask for His will to be done in her life, which is a crucial part of the Lord's Prayer. Seeking God's Kingdom requires not just praising and worshiping Him, but having a personal relationship with Him through Jesus Christ. Therefore, seeking His Kingdom requires His will or His desires for us in life. Yes, we each have our own heart's desires in life, but they have to align with God's will for our lives. As we seek the kingdom and His righteousness, the Spirit of God reveals what God's will is and our specific heart's desires are (Matthew 6:33; Psalm 37:4).

Another time, a man started his prayer by giving thanks to God. Again, he worshiped with wisdom and God was pleased. Then he prayed and the angels received his prayer through his heavenly telephone. They placed his prayer in a golden heavenly bowl then processed his prayer through what appeared to be several offices.

When his prayer reached the last office, I saw the angels open a big drawer, which contained keys. They removed three things and mixed them into the bowl in which this man's prayer was placed. They picked a match box and lit a fire in the golden bowl. The contents were burned. Afterwards, I smelled the sweet aroma of the man's prayer. I wanted to follow the angel holding this golden bowl of sweet, roasted prayers.

One of the higher ranking angels took this bowl and left the space we were occupying. As he walked away, smoke rose from the bowl and ascended to the seat of God Almighty. I saw God was very pleased; this man had prayed well.

I noticed whenever God is pleased with a lifted prayer, the angels pick items from the departments where heavenly goodies are stored. The angels instinctively select such items without command.

Many people do not pray, they simply order God to do what they want. They essentially say, "Lord, I need a car this year. This year won't end before I get it."

This is not really a prayer, it is an order. However, God being the kind of Father He is, overlooks arrogance and grants people their desires, even when a prayer of such caliber is lifted. I also saw the prayers of many go unanswered because they set a time limit on God to provide an answer. People had their own agenda; they did not pray according to His will and timing.

Everything He does is according to His will and strategic programming. For some people, He may determine the car they have prayed for will be given to them as a gift. For others, His plan may be to have them earn or work for it through the sweat of their brow; but he may provide the job or other opportunity through which they will pay for it.

However, there are people whose circumstances have changed by the time God's pre-arranged occurrence for them to get what they prayed for arrives. They are now positioned to receive their blessing. This is why it is important to be at the right place, at the right time.

This requires close consultation with the Spirit of God and walking with God to study the seasons in which our blessings will come. Supporting Scripture in Psalms 37:23 KJV says, "The steps of a good man are ordered by the LORD: and he delighteth in his way." This scriptural reference also means constant obedience and following the commandments of God.

I saw God's angels deliver answered prayers to people, but they did not realize it; they continued praying. On the other hand, I observed angels suffer because they waited for people to whom they were supposed to deliver answered prayers. They could not make the delivery because of their lack of faith.

Unanswered prayer is not due to the angels not being aware of exactly where the recipients of these heavenly gifts are located. Everything must be done decently and in order. When we move away from our rightful position or God's will, we miss our blessing.

I saw angels carrying these delayed gifts. After failing to connect with the recipients, the angels return these gifts to heaven. There are times when God's angels are on their way back to heaven and encounter the devil's angels, who fight them to steal these gifts.

When we pray, we need to remain diligent because our prayers may have already been answered. The things prayed for may already be delivered. In each of these scenarios, Satan has stolen what God has prepared for us, but we have the authority to fight him to recover what he has stolen. We have the power of God to recover anything our enemy the devil has stolen from us, just like King David pursued what the enemy had stolen from him in the book of 1 Samuel 30:8.

Other times, our blessings from God have not been stolen. Instead, the time ordained by God for us to receive a blessing has not yet come (Ecclesiastes 3:1).

Many people complain about how God does not answer their prayers. When I spent my time in heaven, I observed God answer the prayers of every person and creature on earth.

From the time we start thinking of or praying for something, it is granted. Even if we decide to wait on the Lord for the thing we have already prayed and never pray about it again, we will eventually grab a hold of it as long as we are standing in our rightful position in God.

Chapter 19

REPEATING PRAYERS

Another issue about prayer I realized during my time in heaven is they are often repetitive. In and of itself, repeating a prayer several times is not considered out of order. However, if we have prayed a prayer which has reached heaven, angels have already been assigned to deliver it.

I encountered people who pray frequently and intensely; some even spend nights praying. As I took a closer look, I realized these people were not standing on God's word. They were not connected to heaven. A great deal was revealed to me in heaven about prayer. More discussion about this is forthcoming.

You can remind heaven, but it changes nothing. What already has been granted has been set in motion by God, our Provider. Rather, we should thank God for delivering what we have prayed for. It is the core part of the good walk in faith: whatsoever we ask for, we believe we have received, and it shall come to pass.

On the other hand, if we alter our original prayer, it becomes an entirely new prayer, canceling the original prayer altogether. For example, a person may pray for a new car and God ordains him or her to receive it at a specific time the following year. If the person prays for the new car again, he or she has to pray in exactly the same manner as they originally prayed.

If even the slightest change is made, it becomes a new prayer with a new schedule for specified delivery. The person's assigned angels then take his or her prayer through an entirely new process, possibly extending the time it takes to actually secure the new car.

Everything we will ever need on earth is already stored in heaven. When you pray for something and it is granted by God, it becomes the very thing the angels prepare to deliver to you. When we change our original prayer request, it becomes void and sets in motion our altered prayer.

I came upon some people whose prayers were confusing to the angels of God. In these instances, the angels wait to determine exactly what an individual really wants. In heaven, prayers not properly lifted do not reach the ear of God. The angels place these prayers into golden bowls, waiting for what a person prays to be better communicated.

When we properly pray, angels set aside our confused prayers. We need to pray reverently and with wisdom for our requests to reach God for an answer. God is holy; there is no imperfection in Him. We need to approach Him with humility to clearly guide our path.

Whenever anything is incorrectly aligned in our lives, we should recognize that the problem or issue is not God; it is us. We need to check ourselves. Again, in Him there is no imperfection.

After watching various prayer scenarios play out, I wondered why from heaven's vantage point it appears people are not praying at all, whereas on earth people seem to be praying continually. I realized where I had to go for the answer.

As I walked towards the same door I mentioned in Chapter 13 which had opened automatically for the Lord, the angels opened it for me and I entered.

When I stepped inside, I looked down on earth and saw the many pipes, which I told you about in Chapter 17. There is a personal, exclusive pipe through which every person on earth is expected to pray and link to heaven. When we pray, our prayers are routed into these pipes then channeled towards heaven.

At this juncture, I saw exactly where these pipes end. I saw men resembling the mafia—fierce angels of Satan. These murderous, strong demonic spirits were armed with all kinds of weaponry.

These satanic angels hate human beings and their mission is to ensure no prayer passes through to heaven. They are very effective in their work; most prayers do not cross this point. Meaning, heaven does not receive prayers intercepted by satanic angels because they are crushed into ashes.

Satan's angels are not concerned about weak prayers; such prayers simply evaporate or disappear without confrontation. Additionally, when these evil forces do not successfully interfere with lifted prayers, the prayers are weakened as they pass through and disappear without reaching to heaven.

By contrast, I saw other prayers that appeared to be strong travel through these pipes. However, they bounced in and out of these pipes because they were not direct. For a prayer to effectively travel through these pipes, it must be direct and spiritually strong.

Then I viewed some believers who were praying very strong prayers; satanic angels were struggling and fighting against those prayers to destroy them. Some prayers were destroyed, while spiritually strong ones made their way through to heaven.

Then I thought: *Whose prayers can survive these evil men? How on earth can they move past these evil forces?*

A person whose prayer moves past these evil forces must stand in the principles of prayer. Not every person who prays is considered a prayer warrior. In heaven, the people known as prayer warriors adopt certain principles.

The first principle is praying in spirit and truth. The second principle is praying in faith and wisdom. The third principle is praying in the power of the Holy Spirit and holiness.

If a person abides by these principles, satanic angles cannot conquer their prayers because as soon as these prayers are released from the person's mouth (or heart) to enter into his or her pipe leading to heaven, such a prayer is as hot as fire. Evil forces feel the intense heat of such prayers from a great distance. These prayers burn them and force them to withdraw while the prayer warrior's pipe cools.

If our prayers are to make it past the evil forces waiting to destroy them, we have to ensure our prayers are powerful. Equally, it is important for us to pray in wisdom and properly before God.

Another type of prayer I observed at this place of the pipes were prayers that evil forces do not even bother to stop because they are lifted by people who pray as they curse. As these prayers travel uninterrupted, the angels of Satan are excited because they do not go beyond this point.

The angels of Satan implement what these people pray. Meaning, when we are not in proper standing with the Lord, someone may pray against us and the angels of Satan purpose to harm us on his or her behalf.

It is imperative for us to become people of prayer. Even in the church there are people who curse or pray against others. We need to pray with power and in faith. We must walk in holiness and upright with the Lord to protect ourselves against the plots and devices of evil people, witches, and others who would curse us.

It is then that the angels of God are on our side to fight on our behalf. Therefore, it is particularly important to stand on the word of the Lord, so the angels of God will defend us.

Chapter 20

HEAVENLY MANSIONS

In John 14:3 Jesus said, *"And if I go and prepare a place for you, I will come again..."* (KJV). Jesus led me to those places He promised for His followers. He, indeed, prepared these mansions long ago; I saw them.

They are great in number. He prepared and equipped them with the treasures and riches of heaven. They are beautiful beyond description. Since Jesus left the cross at Calvary, He has been preparing places for the human race.

A sad commentary is that Jesus used the greatest treasures and riches to prepare these mansions, but only a small number of people will actually inherit them. The number does not come near half of the world's population.

In heaven, the souls of people arrive as Jesus prepares their mansions. He has continually made preparations for the final wedding. There are times, however, when He steps away from these tasks to make time for His children already residing in heaven—much like a parent takes time to play with their child then resumes his or her duties or work.

I was greatly saddened by the thought of Jesus spending many years to apply every treasure to prepare these places. In my heart I wished Jesus had prepared for only those who will actually enter the heavenly realm, instead of spending all His time and riches preparing so many mansions.

I had no way of knowing, but later learned my thoughts hurt Jesus. He was angry, but He simply lifted my hand and we moved on. As we proceeded, He said nothing.

When Jesus finished preparing places for His followers, He went into the huge heavenly kitchen. Here, He worked with millions of angels, cooking and preparing for an event comparable to a festive and greatly attended wedding ceremony.

From what I saw in the Spirit, without any specific hour being revealed, it was evident the wedding ceremony was fast approaching. As you know, according to scripture, in heaven one day is like a thousand days. Equally, a thousand days are like a day (2 Peter 3:8 KJV). Heaven is not time-bound.

Jesus stood and directed the angels, *"Everyone. Whatever you are doing, do it quickly."* No person was idle.

I was walking with Jesus, but from where I stood, the angels were swirling past me with lightning speed. I had no space to stand, so I exited the heavenly kitchen.

Again, I was disturbed when I saw the billions of angels working at a terrific speed to prepare for the huge party, and all the while their faces were sad. Jesus labored with them in the same manner; this made me weep.

His eyes were extremely tearful; Jesus cried for the many souls for whom He had prepared a place who will never see it. He remembered the bloody price He paid at Calvary's cross; the memories brought Him to tears.

Once again, I reflected on what I was taking in and I felt for Him and the many angels working so hard, laboring for so many years. I saw how hard-working Jesus was and I thought: *I wish He would spare His energy and prepare for only those people who would actually arrive.*

For a second time, Jesus heard my thoughts. However, this time He was extremely annoyed.

He commanded, *"Leave me alone because it is in order for Me to fulfill all righteousness. Let Me do what I am supposed to do because in heaven, we fulfill all righteousness. It's you sons and daughters of men who don't fulfill all righteousness. Let Me do what I am supposed to do because time has run out."*

He continued with His finger pointed at me, *"I'm about to close the door. Now, this is what I am going to do—I am going to close the door. I will forgive those I will forgive."*

Chapter 21

A Taste of the Gehenna Fires

When Jesus pointed His finger at me saying, *"I will forgive whom I will forgive,"* I felt a mighty force rush through my body and I fell down. I immediately felt immense heat and fire. The force started pushing me backwards—I was helpless and had nothing to hold onto.

The force pushed me towards a huge valley. The farther I tumbled, the more intense the heat became. The force of Jesus' words pushed me a space equal in distance from Uganda to London. It was very far down the valley, towards a deep pit.

As I tumbled farther down this valley, I began to sense I was seated in a very hot place. I realized this place was called Gehenna, the lake of fire; the bottomless pit of hell. However, I was not actually inside hell, but I was suspended in mid-air, directly above its realm.

The fire burned me terribly. I started to weep like the inhabitants of Gehenna, who were crying. This fire burns so fiercely, there is nothing comparable to it in this world. You cannot imagine it.

My entire being was on fire from the inside of the bone and marrow, meat, muscles—everywhere. I started calling for Jesus, but whenever I cried out His name, I felt like another load of fire had been poured into my mouth.

As I continued to call out Jesus' name, another load of fire was poured into my mouth; I felt I was dying. Whenever I opened my mouth, more fire would be poured into it. I continued to burn from within. There are no words to describe the pain inflicted by these fires of hell.

In Gehenna, there are so many people, like sand on the seashore. All of them were black and burnt to a crisp, like trees burned after a bush fire.

Although this fire burns terribly, it does not entirely consume a person. When a person is nearly consumed, they recover to their original form just prior to entering Gehenna. The fire starts burning the person afresh, through the same process, until once again he/she nearly becomes consumed. The same process occurs repeatedly.

This is what people who have been relegated to hell go through daily. Yet, they do not die. They are alive and fully understand they are in hell, remembering all too well everything they did on earth.

I saw them passing judgment on themselves for going to Gehenna. Some lamented, "Why did we end up in this place?" or "Indeed, I was the guilty one."

They often cried and suffered dehydration. Hell's fire drains a person to experience total dryness. Yet there is not a single drop of water available.

Suffering extreme thirst, I cried for water like the inhabitants. As I was agonizing in great pain, a certain angel came along dressed in bright white attire. He pulled me out of Gehenna then returned me to Jesus.

Still quite angry, Jesus said, *"I will forgive whom I will forgive."*

Jesus is so good, but He also can be very tough. He is very kind, but He also can be very stern. Jesus heals, but He also can destroy. Whatever His demeanor, He is absolute in it. He can be a great, yet harsh friend.

He said, *"You have found mercy in my eyes. Let this be an example for you when you return to the world and fail to do what you have been instructed."*

Then, as instantaneously as His fury, He forgave me. Once again, He led me by the hand and we moved on.

Chapter 22

ABRAHAM'S PALACE

After we left the kitchen, Jesus departed from me for awhile. I walked out of the city of God, surrounded by a huge fence. I exited through another door and passed through the courtyard. Then I came across another gate where the palace of Abraham is located.

Near the entrance, I met two people who had died and just arrived from earth. When we reached the gate, they opened it and I heard them exclaim, "He is the one! He is our grandfather, Abraham!"

They ran towards a certain individual with such excitement. I wondered who they were talking about. Then I saw Abraham from a distance seated under a beautiful shade on a beautiful chair in very bright colors.

This is the reason why every person who reaches him says, "He is the one." It is as if you already know him. You understand him, even if you have never seen him.

With equal excitement, I also ran towards him behind the two people I had encountered at the entrance. Abraham is seated in front of his palace, waiting to receive every person who made it to heaven.

When people arrive in heaven, they do not initially see God Almighty. They go to Abraham's palace where he awaits their arrival to receive them. When I reached him, I sat on his lap and touched his short beard, which is as bright as the sun.

Abraham is a handsome man; he is neither old nor young. His body was very bright, very soft. He looked wonderful. We were enjoying every moment we rested our heads on his chest.

To his left and right are elders whose task is to lead people away once he has received them. At times, the elders are required to forcibly pull people away.

The elders led me and the two new arrivals away; they were directed to enter further into Abraham's palace. However, I was not taken any further because I was scheduled to return to earth.

As I looked inside, I saw many people dressed in white who lived with Abraham.

I heard them asking, "Who is that? Who has come in?"

I did not want to leave the palace to return to earth. I was very sad to be taken from Abraham's arms. Impulsively, I struggled with the elders as they led me away.

They escorted me away from Abraham's palace to the gate. I slowly returned to the city of God. As I was walked, I eventually was reunited with Jesus. He led me by the hand towards the seat of God Almighty.

Jesus and I approached the front of God's seat. Jesus humbled Himself before God Almighty and said, *"Aida, this is God, our Father."*

Jesus ushered me towards His right then He walked towards God. He stood before God with His head bowed, demonstrating deep respect and honor.

God Almighty was extremely bright; golden colors beamed from Him. In the midst of this brightness, I saw His massive golden garment, flowing throughout heaven. I saw His garment but was not able to look directly at Him due to His extreme brightness.

As Jesus led me towards God's chair, my eyes could not be opened. My head was bent at knee level. However, even with closed eyes and a bent head, His glory penetrated through my being.

When I stood before God's presence, He wanted to speak to me, but I could not speak to Him. Therefore, He hid His glory. Still, I could not look at Him. So, He left His chair and came down the sparkling white staircase. He stood four steps from where we were.

He declared, *"Aida, you have received favor in my eyes; I am God Almighty. You are going to go back to the world and tell the people I am God Almighty. Go and tell all the people I am holy; let them also be holy. Tell all the people they should worship Me in spirit and in truth. Tell all the people to obey My word. Tell all the people to ascend to My holy mountain because only those who will do it will come to heaven."*

He continued, *"Tell them to do it quickly because only those who will do it will come to heaven."*

Once more, He said, *"Only those who will ascend My holy mountain are the ones who will make it to heaven."*

The issue of ascending God's holy mountain, as revealed to me in the Spirit, does not encompass merely climbing earthly hills or mountains. Ascending God's holy mountain means seeking the Lord with all our heart, soul, strength, power, and understanding. It means sacrificing our lives to Him, giving Him everything we have, seeking Him in holiness, obeying His word, and separating ourselves from the world to fellowship with Him.

It may even mean losing everything—doing it in pursuit of Him. It means knowing and seeking God, like a person searches for a treasure. This is what it means to ascend the Lord's holy mountain.

God made it very clear who will enter heaven. Then he smiled and bid me farewell, climbing the white stairway to return to His seat. At this point, Jesus emerged from where He had been standing.

He took my hand, walked me through different parts of heaven. We strolled leisurely and appeared to be climbing a hill. We continued to climb until we reached what seemed to be the end of heaven.

Chapter 23

THREADLIKE BRIDGE

Heaven and earth are separated by a huge valley as large as the universe itself. A threadlike bridge, incomparable to bridges on earth, links heaven and earth. This bridge spans the valley (Gehenna), which is as wide as the entire world. In order to reach heaven, every person must cross this bridge. There is no other route.

There are three places, namely heaven, earth, and this valley (Gehenna). Let no person be deceived—only heaven, earth, and Gehenna exist. When we leave this world, we will either go to heaven or hell. However, we have to cross this bridge to reach heaven. If we fail to do so, we fall into Gehenna.

As I walked with Jesus on golden roads toward the end of heaven, we reached this tiny, threadlike bridge and started to descend. The valley it bridged is bottomless, dark, and filled with murky, foul water.

Jesus led me across this bridge. When we reached its end, we came upon a place resembling the seashore. This area of the bridge was extremely busy. I sensed the Holy Spirit was at this place because He helps people cross this bridge.

Although the Holy Spirit was present and tried to help, millions of people fell from this threadlike bridge into Gehenna nearly every second. They could not cross this bridge for a number of reasons which I will later explain.

There appeared to be small holes, the size dug by ants and insects. Thousands of people emerged from these holes from earth onto the bridge leading to heaven. Some came through small paths while others traveled along bigger ones.

People came from various pathways in large numbers. Yet, all fell into Gehenna. It was extremely frightening and brought me to tears.

In this life, every person has to choose where they want to spend eternity. I learned this kind of judgment was already made. By the time the threadlike bridge is reached no judgment remains; there is no possibility of asking questions or getting near God.

Every person who leaves this world reaches the place where he/she will ultimately reside for eternity. People who refuse to receive Jesus as their personal Lord and Savior have already been judged and know their fate.

As it is written: *"He that believeth on him is not condemned: but he that believeth not is condemned already..."* (John 3:18 KJV).

This statement is materially critical to this overall message. As a prerequisite of entering heaven, one must accept Christ as his or her personal Savior and believe He is the Son of God (Romans 10:9–10; John 3:3). I even saw born-again believers who fell from this bridge into the valley for a variety of reasons:

- First, I saw many born-again Christians who had carried heavy burdens in their minds, on their backs, in bags, and in both hands. (Remember, this bridge is like a thread and a believer cannot cross over it heavy laden.) Yet, the Holy Spirit spoke to them day and night to help relieve their burdens, but these people did not let Him.

- I observed a second cluster of people who, on the surface, looked good, but deep inside their hearts were morally corrupt and unpleasant. So much so, parts fell off their rotted hearts. Such people cannot cross this bridge either.

- There was a third category of people who possessed small hearts. These Christians looked outwardly good, but their bodies were covered with very sharp swords.

- The swords represented sharp words, bad thoughts, hearts not filled with love, but rather hatred (four swords in hearts).

Murderers carried sharp swords in their hands and, in one way or another, had committed the spiritual and/or physical hurt or murder against others. Such people pierce and wound every person who comes into their midst. These kinds of people cannot cross the bridge.

- A fourth group included people who waited on the Lord but did not worship God in spirit and truth. They had not understood the seasons of the Lord—sowing and expecting a harvest in due season like a hardworking farmer. As part of the requirement to receive rewards from the Lord in heaven, we must worship Him in truth and in spirit. We all reap what we sow. And in due season, all that wait upon the Lord and do as the word says will be strengthened (John 4:23-24, Isaiah 40:31, Ecclesiastes 3:1, Gal 6:9). Born-again Christians who did not worship in truth and spirit also fell into the dark valley.

- A fifth type of person was troubled in his thoughts by the cares and concerns of this world. He worries about finances and debts, children, and a host of other things. The Holy Spirit had been speaking to these people, trying to help them, but they would not let Him. They continued worrying over the things of this world, and this pulled them further away from God's presence.

- A sixth kind of person was lame beyond description. On the exterior, they appear to be normal, but they are crippled in spirit.

- Seventh, were people who were blind and deaf. These people could neither sense the Holy Spirit's presence nor hear what He was saying to them. Again, such people fell off the threadlike bridge to perish in Gehenna.

- Other people had bad hearts. This eighth group was filled with hatred, malice, envy, and unforgiveness. They were confrontational, unholy, godless, and absent an intimate relationship with God.

- I saw others who were considered heavy in spirit but light in the body. Meaning, it was very hard for them to do the things of God, but very easy for them to do carnal things. This ninth group succeeded in crossing this bridge because they were light in the spirit, not the flesh.

- Some of the few people who managed to cross this bridge into heaven appeared to be dead. They were dead in the flesh, but alive in the spirit. This tenth category was so united with the Holy Spirit that He covered them completely. Such people were so attuned to the Holy Spirit they obeyed simple instructions, only doing what He directed them to do. These people crossed this bridge with ease. I watched them walk as the Holy Spirit led them.

- I saw an eleventh group comprised of children who had died during childbirth. These infants arrived with their mothers. These babies actually walked, following their mothers; however, they were not aware of one another. All of them looked to the Holy Spirit to help them cross over.

- Finally, there were children who were aborted. I saw them crawl and their mothers were unaware of their existence. It is a very complex picture.

Navigating this threadlike bridge is very difficult. Every person is personally responsible for successfully crossing it; only the Holy Spirit can help. There are people who neglect the Holy Spirit, hoping to turn to

Him when they arrive at this bridge. We must leave this world walking with Him if He is to help us cross this bridge.

When we arrive at the bridge, there is a supernatural power already within us which unites with the power of the Holy Spirit at the bridge. It is this combined force which propels us across the bridge. If we arrive without this supernatural power, we fall into the valley of Gehenna.

Additionally, if we do not carefully listen to the step-by-step instructions issued by the Holy Spirit as we cross this bridge, we fall into Gehenna, without any hope of returning.

Chapter 24

CHILDREN PERISHING

After my observations at the bridge leading into heaven, Jesus said, *"Aida, come."*

As He held my hand, we walked up to the bridge's central point. He asked, *"Have you seen those things?"*

I looked into the bottomless valley and He said, *"This is the world of Satan, Gehenna, where My people perish. But I want you to go back to the world; this is very urgent. Tell the people on earth to help the young children greatly. The young children are perishing."*

I saw young children falling into the valley of Gehenna. They tried to navigate the thin bridge, but eventually fell. Why do these seemingly innocent children perish? Because within them there is no seed of God's word.

Therefore, the Lord told me to go back to the world and tell the people the children are perishing. These children range in age from infants to those who attend colleges and universities. They are all perishing. This task is the responsibility of every person on earth.

Jesus instructed me to tell every person on earth, *"The children are perishing at a terrific rate; they should help the children. Satan has hatched a plan to steal children so rapidly. Go and tell all people to preach the Gospel to the children, take them to the churches, teach them how to fear the Lord and to know Him, and teach them the word of God to help them in every way, for many are not cared for."*

He continued, *"Go and tell them to help the children, and to do it very quickly."*

Now I am telling this to you. It is a responsibility of everybody, for the Lord said so.

As I continued my tour, I saw people who were travelling through villages and towns. They were looking for children from babies to those who studied in higher education institutions, preaching the gospel.

The Lord is asking us to help children and we should do it very quickly. For this is the responsibility of every person.

It is fitting to examine ourselves to determine if our lives are aligned with God to cross this bridge. We need to be light in the spirit, and heavy in the body. In other words, we must be a people who find it easy to do the things of God, yet hard to do the things of the flesh.

Our lives need to serve as a witness to children who are perishing. They need to know about Satan's plan for their lives to ultimately prevent them from successfully crossing the bridge into heaven.

Chapter 25

THE HIGHWAY

Then Jesus and I descended this bridge to the world toward the Highway of Salvation. This highway spans from the end of the earth to the bridge entering heaven. In other words, apart from the other small paths and holes through which people also poured onto the bridge from earth, this Highway of Salvation is the most direct route leading into heaven.

On this highway are many things. First and foremost, the people on this highway are supposed to be born-again Christians. Yet, people on this highway represent criminal mafias, who are no different than the people outside of this highway.

The Highway of Salvation is filled with terror, like other places in a fallen world. There is a lot of madness, confusion, violence, murder, gossip, and every other immoral practice imaginable. Some people on this highway are agents of Satan, who also are moving along. They are killers armed with swords, piercing others.

The people who traveled this highway should have been ready for combat. These people have been given full combat gear and the necessary weaponry of soldiers. However, they are not dressed in full combat gear. Indeed, these people are soldiers, not meant to fight one another. There is a common enemy, armed and dressed for battle.

However, some people were seated idly while others looked attentive, yet confused. They did not know what they were supposed to be doing. They had been given full combat uniforms, but were very weak. They did nothing.

Most people I saw were half-dressed in shirts and no trouser or vice versa. These people prayed carnal prayers using the word of God. Such people are considered spiritually half-dressed in the eyes of God. Some had guns but no shoes; while others with pangas, a symbol depicting the sword of the Spirit originally meant to serve to the glory of God, used them to slay each other.

Christians are supposed to wear the full armor of God (Ephesians 6:10–18). What I saw, however, portrayed a Christian community half-dressed spiritually. One has faith, but is not walking righteously. Another has the sword of the Spirit—the word of the Lord— yet he does not have the helmet of salvation.

Interestingly, each thought they were walking fully with God as Christians, whereas they were missing one or more of the necessary weapons to fight the enemy. Christians today are spending more time fighting each other than fighting the common enemy, Satan.

The Highway of Salvation is comprised of many people with different measures of strength. Some have already fallen by the wayside and appear to be dead. There are others who seem to have some degree of strength, but they are so weak they find it hard to breathe. They simply crawl on the ground. Such people need someone to help carry them until they are able to continue the journey under their own strength.

Oddly enough, those able to muster a bit of strength attack those who have less strength. They hit them with iron bars and pierce their hearts with swords. They kill them and discard them completely.

I saw others who appeared to be strong, but they trampled over others to get ahead. Similar to when someone sees his neighbor getting ahead of him, instead of trying to learn from his success and rolling up his sleeves, he searches for a big stone to hit him over the head, causing him to fall behind. Then this person, after removing the other person, tries to occupy his position.

I saw very weak people and thought they would help one another, but even the weak were undermining each other. Again, I saw jealousy, stealing, violence, murder, and evil on the Highway of Salvation.

There are also many angels on the highway; however, the people traveling this way do not know they are present. As a result, these angels do not work. Each angel stands in their position, but does nothing. They observe the people. What can the angels do for them? So, the angels look on until the end of time when they are withdrawn or re-deployed by God.

I also saw the Holy Spirit there, trying to help the people. However, people are unwilling to be helped; they do not hear and are deaf. They also blindly move up and down. There are so many interesting things to observe on this highway.

Again, the people on the Highway of Salvation were soldiers; there was not a single civilian. They are all designed to be fighters, strong fighters. These people are on the frontline, facing an enemy, but what is disturbing is some of these people sleep while others fight one another.

Now, because they are so confused and unsure of what to do, the enemy infiltrates their ranks and fiercely attacks—leaving many dead, broken, and taken captive.

This highway was flanked by two strong, high walls on either side. The highway and the people who walked it could be safe if they were where they were supposed to be. Like any highway, if you follow the traffic rules you save yourself from getting killed in any accidents. There are some dangerous highway robbers, kidnappers, as well as reckless drivers—some with DUI records—out there. Some drivers simply don't follow traffic rules; others go the wrong way. While the highway to heaven is designed to be a straight road to heaven in the Christian and spiritual world, so to speak, we don't do what we ought to do and end up hurting other fellow born-again Christians. Even as we call ourselves born-again Christians living for Christ, many continue to harbor unforgiveness, murder, hatred, malice, gossip and the like, even in Church. It is these abuses that fill the highway to heaven with terror. Also, there are wolves in sheepskins within the Church. The word of God says even Satan is transformed into an angel of light (2 Corinthians 11:14). That's why many don't make it to heaven. The road to heaven is a very narrow pathway (Matthew 7:13).

On either side of these walls are strong armies of Satan, well-prepared to fight. They have all the weapons they need. However, the people in the way are not ready for combat, they are not armed. They do not know who they are fighting. The people have spent a great deal of time fighting one another; therefore, the armies of Satan take advantage of the situation.

When I walked with Jesus, He told me to share the following message. However, before I release what He commanded, I need to explain why.

I was serving in my church choir when fellow believers lodged false accusations against me. They treated me badly and broke my heart. There was a lot of gossip to contend with and people talked behind my back. I felt ashamed and carried a wounded heart. By the time of my death experience when I ascended to heaven, I felt as if I was accusing my accusers before Jesus.

Like me, there are many of you who have been wounded in this way. This is the reason Jesus directed me to share these words.

He said, *"Listen, all you ends of the earth; look to God and get saved. If you look to sons of men, you won't succeed."*

He added, *"Don't be upset by sons of men because not every person you see in the church is a Christian. Not everyone who praises the Lord is born-again. Not every person who serves in the Church is a believer."*

There are two ways: life and death. There are two places: heaven and hell. It is up to us to choose; what we sow is what we reap. Whatever we do, we need to do it with all our heart.

If the decision is to change, then change for the better. If the decision is to receive salvation, then be fully saved. If the decision is to live holy, then live holy. If the decision is to obey the Word of God, then obey it fully. If we choose to give, then we must give with all our heart.

This is the time for everyone to do whatever they are doing with all their heart; the rewards are full and real. Do not blame God for the misbehavior of people, for this grieves God. Let every person know who called him/her. Let every person do what he/she is assigned to do. It grieves God if we mistreat one another and cause fellow believers to abandon the good things they are supposed to be doing.

Concerning the church, Jesus explained there are different departments. What did He mean? If we see someone performing certain duties then we know under which department this person falls.

The church is comprised of the following types of people, representing various departments:

- Individuals who have recited the salvation prayer, but never truly received Jesus into their hearts. Such people are not saved; in this world they may be seen as very powerful, but heaven does not recognize them.

- People who have truly accepted Jesus as their Lord and Savior, but do not obey what He tells them to do; therefore, heaven doesn't know them well. When we respond to the call and accept Jesus as our Lord and Savior, and earnestly repent for our sins, every person is considered blameless and given two minutes of perfect holiness. From this point, everyone is accountable to work out his or her holiness.

- Jesus told me the most active department is comprised of those who gossip. This activity has destroyed many, sending them into Gehenna. He said, *"Go to the world and tell them I am displeased with gossip. It's like smoke billowing out day and night, which has reached My presence. Go tell them I am displeased with gossiping in the church!"*

- There are believers who were saved, but do not worship the Lord in spirit and in truth. Although they have given up everything for the Lord and have also suffered much for the Lord, they do not understand the seasons of the Lord; therefore, they do not worship the Lord in spirit and in truth.

- There are those who are confused, who have left or given up everything for the Lord. They have suffered for the Lord, and are waiting on the Lord. However, they do not know the seasons of the Lord and are, therefore, filled with fear and worry over the affairs of this world. Such worry and anxiety draws them away from the presence of the Lord; they end up confused and disturbed.

- Finally, there are people who say they are waiting on the Lord, but they do not understand Him. They do not understand the Holy Spirit either. They do not understand the seasons of the Lord, thinking there is yet more time, whereas time has already run out.

Continue to seek God and work out your own salvation. This is the time for everyone to know God personally, and to choose who they will follow. Unfortunately, many people are confused.

As Jesus and I continued our walk, we went to a place where people were praying overnight.

Jesus asked. *"Who allowed these people to come and spoil my courts?"*

The reason Jesus said this was because despite the fact that there is abundant and sufficient grace out there for everyone, especially those who have accepted Christ as their personal savior, many still carry heavy loads, filled with fear and worry as though they are still in bondage. Jesus has asked everyone to give all their burdens and cares to him in Matthew 11:28.

For instance, fear is not of the Lord. Where there is fear there is no Love and yet God is Love. So if you fear, you don't believe God is well able (1 John 4:7–8). In a way it portrays that He died for nothing. He wants us to have the love, peace, joy, kindness and all that he has planned for us. He wants us to love one another as we love ourselves and show the same kindness, peace, etc. as accorded to us through Him, to all our fellow human beings. The reverse is happening even among those who are considered children of God and are called by His name. This shows that many still don't understand Him up to now or simply don't have enough faith, thus spoiling His Courts. "Without faith it is impossible to please God" (Hebrews 11:6 KJV).

He encouraged us not to be discouraged by fellow Christians, but to move steadfastly toward the attainment of the crown of glory awaiting all who overcome and make it to the very end.

We are the temple of the Holy Spirit (1 Corinthians 3:16). Yet, as members of the sacred body of Christ, we have made our minds, hearts, and bodies a haven for all kinds of evil filled with envy, hatred, anger, lies, and murder toward each other; against the nature and word of God; and displeasing to Jesus, who died that we may be saved.

It is not too late to repent and return to God even after falling. No sin is so great it cannot be forgiven by God. He is a God full of loving kindness and tender mercies.

As the Bible urges, now is the time for everyone to return to their first love and walk the way of peace. Let everyone return to his or her original path from where he/she has gone astray.

I have seen people who proudly proclaim they have been born again for forty years. This tendency to testify about forty years of salvation is an ideal of Christendom which is no longer valid. In those forty years, their walk in holiness may be equivalent to two minutes. This means they had never truly been saved; heaven does not recognize them.

Others may testify they have been born again for ten years. The question becomes: during those ten years, how long have you lived holy? The time we have spent walking in holiness is what really counts in heaven.

Now, with regard to serving in church ministries, every person has his or her own ministry in which he/she has been called by God to serve. Some of these ministries include working in an office environment, while others require participating in a ministry which contributes to Sunday morning worship. Every person is responsible for bringing in his or her tithes and offerings, and praise and worship to the Lord in the beauty of holiness.

Unless we fulfill the work predestined in our heavenly file, we will not have done what we were created to do. We have done good works, but not what we were sent to earth to do.

Some people are called to be entrepreneurs. God blesses them so they will bring money into the church to promote the work of God. This may be their ministry, not necessarily pastoring a church. However, the church is in a state of confusion as pastors are becoming businessmen and businessmen have started pastoring churches.

Whatever the Holy Spirit is leading you to do, this may be your calling. Some people are called to be physicians, while others are assigned to be singers. Some people are called to be pastors, while others are assigned to be philanthropists.

When I was in heaven, I saw some people who were called to be helpers planted in the church to lend a hand to those who are distressed, destitute, and helpless. There are some people who God has called to minister love to people.

For example, someone may come to the church at the point of wanting to commit suicide, or with a distraught heart. Someone else's calling may be to restore strength and hope to such a person. As the distressed person is being helped, he or she comes to know God really cares and can eventually walk victoriously in the way of salvation. An act of kindness, as simple as a smile shown to such a person, may be enough to change the course of his or her life.

Anything that builds up the Body of Christ, God has assigned someone to it. From sweeping the church corridor to evangelizing throughout neighboring communities, someone has been called to do it. Such a person is considered a minister of God.

Some people are created to conduct door-to-door evangelism, but *they* have decided to pastor a church instead. Others become pastors when God has not actually called them; such people may create problems with far-reaching effects.

A pastor is equipped with a spirit of parental love for his or her sheep, requiring nurturing and a guiding spirit. However, if a pastor causes division among his or her sheep, this person may not be operating in his or her proper calling. Such a person must discover where God created him/her to be, then take his or her rightful position.

There are many people whom God actually called to be evangelists, so they can bring souls into the church where pastors nurture those souls. However, such people often pastor churches instead of evangelizing. There is a lot of confusion, as everyone is now doing what they want rather than what God called them to do.

I have seen people stand in their rightful positions. It takes strength to stand where God has called us because there will be people who try to beat, knock, or pull us down from where God has placed us. It is our responsibility to fight and stand firm as we claim our rightful position.

There are so many ministries or callings designated within the church; God will reward those who serve Him. Every person will be crowned, according to his or her faithfulness in doing what he/she is called to do. Every person will be asked to account for every word spoken. When you leave this world, you may find a good report in heaven.

Chapter 26

HEAVENLY MONITORS

The next thing I saw in heaven were monitors similar to movie screens. Each person on earth has a monitor in heaven to capture every movement we make, everywhere we go, and every act we commit.

I was in awe of how the monitors recorded everything daily. As I marveled, I was shown my personal reel. I saw every step I had ever taken, including every word I had ever spoken. There were some things I did not remember happening; therefore, I found it hard to accept I had done them in such places. I saw myself uttering words I did not remember ever saying.

These monitors are designed to capture our activities from the time we began to think clearly as children to the time we depart from earth. As I continued to watch my reel, I experienced fear and panic, similar to when I watch an intense football game and a rival team is close to scoring.

As I viewed my heavenly monitor, I reacted aloud, anticipating my stumble or fall in certain circumstances. I cheered at circumstances when I was victorious.

I realized no angels operated the screens. I was left alone to view my life on earth. After I finished watching, I was directed by what I had seen to another place. Others who had viewed their individual screens were there as well.

One day everyone will view their monitor then pass on to either heaven or hell, knowing he/she deserved his or her final place of verdict. Wherever our final resting place, we know heavenly monitors are recording every single act we commit or thought we think during our lives; it will be replayed on the day we depart earth.

After viewing my monitor, I perceived I am victorious. I am worthy to be granted a place in heaven. What actually made me recognize I am victorious? The treasure revealed to me in Chapter 7.

I was among people who had access to this particular treasure as a result of believing in and remaining committed to God. It is the greatest heavenly treasure, which shines brightly with so much glory. It reflects even more than the light of one thousand suns.

Inside this treasure were riches greater than the caches of this world. A heavenly computer scanned my right hand—I found this treasure to reside within me. As a result, I was granted my place in heaven.

Chapter 27
THE FINAL CALL

Just then, I heard a humble, soft voice calling, *"Aida, although you have vacated [your] earthly life, there is a job you did not complete and, therefore, you need to go back to earth and complete it."*

I replied I did not want to go back; I was happy where I was, and at that point I did not regret forsaking the work I was supposed to complete. At the time, I was unaware of the importance or significance of what I was being called to do. Now I know that I was created specifically for this purpose: to be the medium through which this message from God would be brought to the rest of the world, so that others may know that there is a heaven and hell in the afterlife.

I was one who had not accomplished her assigned work. What was painful? Whenever those of us who had not accomplished our earthly assignments saw Jesus, we would run away from Him like we were running away from a lion determined to devour us.

Indeed there is everlasting perfect joy in heaven for those who have accomplished their earthly works. Those who had not carried out their assignments were looking for a place to hide, which saddened me since I believed Jesus was my only and best friend.

I began questioning why I was beginning to run from Jesus. However, the Holy Spirit reminded me I had not accomplished the job I was supposed to do here on earth. It was a final call by God to accomplish the task I was called to do. And that's how I reconnected to the voice of Pastor Simeone Kayiwa across the sea and came back to earth to fulfill this God-given task.

Epilogue

Many Christian believers continue to search for truth through the Word of God. It is my humble submission that the Bible continues to be the source of truth.

The experience I had during my death and restoration—the brief journey to heaven and the actual witnessing of hell—and all I learned from God Almighty; our Lord and Savior, Jesus Christ; as well as the Holy Spirit, is a confirmation of truth, as told in the Bible.

I would humbly ask everyone who has read the message in this book to take it seriously and follow everything taught in the Bible. It is only through confessing by mouth and believing in our hearts that Jesus is the Son of God (Romans 10:9–10)—sent to die on the cross, resurrected on the third day, and ascended into heaven—along with asking for the forgiveness of our sins, forgiving others, walking with Christ, praying daily, and accepting Jesus as our Savior, that we can partake in the kingdom of God and have eternal life.

It is my hope this book will strengthen your faith and help you walk in faith and righteousness through Jesus Christ. Most importantly, God is love and without love no one will be able to see Him. He requires our relationship with one another—individual to individual as well as between nations—be based on love (Luke 10:27).

God desires for us to seek Him and do everything according to His will and what He has purposed for our lives. May God richly bless you.

Remarks

You are very fortunate to read these words. However, you are in peril if you read them and refuse or neglect to do what they are telling you to do. May God richly bless you with an overflow!

Biography

Aidah N. Nakasujja Nsereko is a born-again Christian who was born in 1978 to parents Anna Nankya and Bethel Kayiira at Bombo Hospital, Ndejje Bombo. She studied at Anoonya Jerusalem Primary School up to primary six, which is the equivalent of fifth grade in the United States.

She recently married Mr. David Nsereko and has been a member of Namirembe Christian Fellowship in Kampala, Uganda, under the leadership of Pastor Simeone Kayiwa. Along with being a member of the church's choir, Aidah is a gifted interpreter of dreams.

After the 2006 incident during which she died for a period of about nine hours and was revived by the power of God Almighty and our lord Jesus Christ, she became a full-time evangelist. She currently preaches the gospel in various villages within the rural region where peasants are frequently impoverished. They are not only in desperate need physically, but are also hungry for the Word of God.

Aidah epitomizes the fulfillment of her call to teach the Good News to all nations (Matthew 28:19–20). She has traveled in various parts of East Africa, but mainly within Uganda. She has dedicated her life to spreading God's word through evangelism as directed by the Lord in Matthew 24:14.